Super Simple
Cultural Art

Super Simple
MEXICAN ART

Fun and Easy Art from Around the World

Alex Kuskowski

Consulting Editor, Diane Craig, M.A./Reading Specialist

A Division of ABDO
ABDO
Publishing Company

visit us at www.abdopublishing.com

Published by ABDO Publishing Company, a division of ABDO, P.O. Box 398166, Minneapolis, Minnesota 55439. Copyright © 2012 by Abdo Consulting Group, Inc. International copyrights reserved in all countries. No part of this book may be reproduced in any form without written permission from the publisher. Super SandCastle™ is a trademark and logo of ABDO Publishing Company.

Printed in the United States of America, North Mankato, Minnesota
102011
012012

 PRINTED ON RECYCLED PAPER

Editor: Liz Salzmann
Content Developer: Nancy Tuminelly
Interior Design and Production: Oona Gaarder-Juntti, Mighty Media, Inc.
Cover Design: Kelsey Gullickson, Mighty Media, Inc.
Photo Credits: Jack Hollingsworth, Shutterstock, Thinkstock

The following manufacturers/names appearing in this book are trademarks: Elmer's® Glue-All™, Glitter Glue™, Hershey's®, Kit Kat®. Mod Podge®, Peter Paul® Almond Joy®, Reese's® Peanut Butter Cups®, Scotch®, Scribbles®, Sharpie®

Library of Congress Cataloging-in-Publication Data

Kuskowski, Alex.
  Super simple Mexican art : fun and easy art from around the world / Alex Kuskowski.
    p. cm. -- (Super simple cultural art)
  ISBN 978-1-61783-213-0
  1. Handicraft--Mexico--Juvenile literature. 2. Decorative arts--Mexico--Juvenile literature. 3. Arts, Mexican--Juvenile literature. I. Title.
  TT28.K87 2012
  745.50972--dc23
                          2011024605

Super SandCastle™ books are created by a team of professional educators, reading specialists, and content developers around five essential components—phonemic awareness, phonics, vocabulary, text comprehension, and fluency—to assist young readers as they develop reading skills and strategies and increase their general knowledge. All books are written, reviewed, and leveled for guided reading, early reading intervention, and Accelerated Reader® programs for use in shared, guided, and independent reading and writing activities to support a balanced approach to literacy instruction.

TO ADULT HELPERS

Children can have a lot of fun learning about different cultures through arts and crafts. Be sure to supervise them as they work on the projects in this book. Let the kids do as much as possible on their own. But be ready to step in and help if necessary. Also, kids may be using glue, paint, markers, and clay. Make sure they protect their clothes and work surfaces.

Table of Contents

Day of the Dead

The Day of the Dead is a special Mexican holiday. It is a time to remember family members who have died.

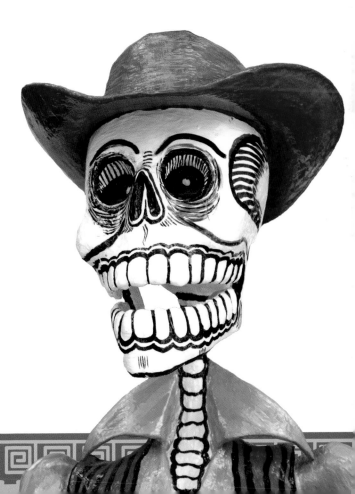

Art Around the World

People from around the world do things differently. That's because of their **culture**. Everyone belongs to a culture, even you! Learning about different cultures can be a lot of fun.

Each culture has its own way of doing things. Often the things the people make show a certain style. Try some of the art projects in this book. See what you can learn about Mexican culture! You can even share what you learn with others.

Before You Start

Remember to treat other people and **cultures** with respect. Respect their art, **jewelry**, and clothes too. These things can have special meaning to people.

There are a few rules for doing art projects.

- **Permission**
  Make sure to ask permission to do a project. You might want to use things you find around the house. Ask first!

- **Safety**
  Get help from an adult when using something hot or sharp. Never use an oven by yourself.

Hojalata

Hojalata is tin art that is made in Mexico. The artists press, cut, and decorate sheets of tin. They make ornaments and wall hangings.

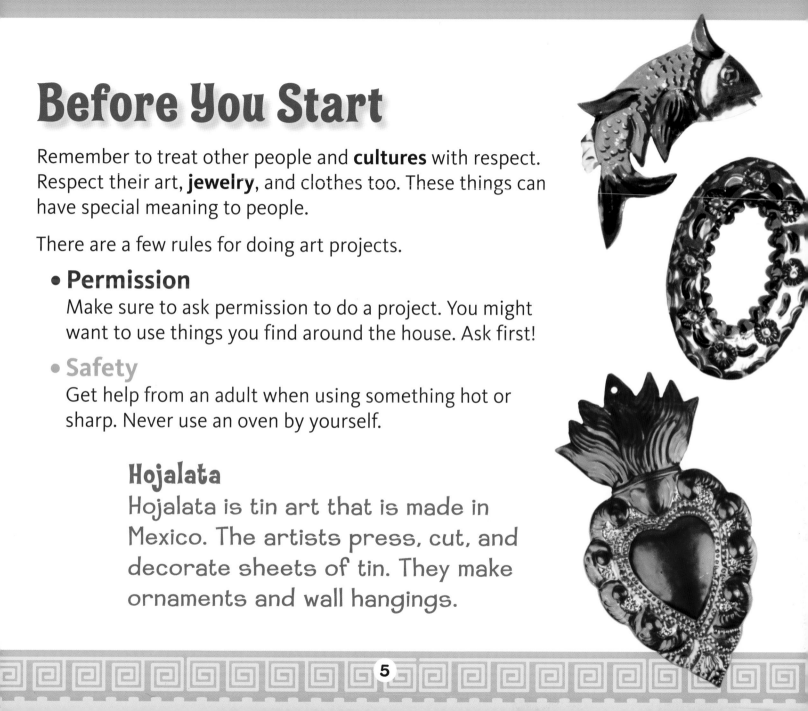

Art in Mexican Culture

People in Mexico create many beautiful things. Some are for everyday use. Others are for special occasions. The **designs** in Mexican art often have special meanings.

Piñata

Piñatas are made out of **papier-mâché**. They are brightly colored and filled with treats. There are piñatas at most Mexican parties.

Paper Flowers
Paper flowers are used at a lot of Mexican holiday parties. From Cinco de Mayo to the Day of the Dead, they're everywhere!

Aztec Sun
The most important **Aztec** god was the sun god. Suns are often found in Mexican art.

Materials

Here are some of the materials you'll need to get started.

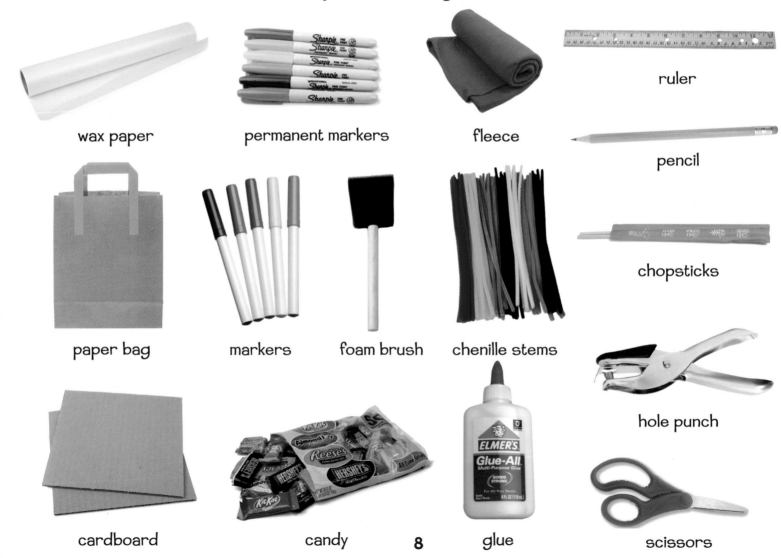

wax paper

permanent markers

fleece

ruler

pencil

paper bag

markers

foam brush

chenille stems

chopsticks

hole punch

cardboard

candy

8

glue

scissors

craft foam

felt

bowls, different sizes

Mod Podge

yarn

aluminum pan

string

masking tape

puffy paint

newspaper

glitter glue

construction paper

tissue paper

stapler **9**

decorative gems

jump rings

GOD'S EYE

The Huichol people make these to show that God is watching over them.

WHAT YOU NEED
- chopsticks
- yarn
- scissors
- glue

1. Put one of the sticks on top of the other. They should cross in the middle. Tie the end of the yarn around the sticks.

2. Wrap the yarn around the sticks. Wrap it each way a few times. This holds the sticks together.

3. Hold the sticks where they cross. Wrap the yarn under and around one of the sticks. Push the wrapped yarn together on the stick. Pull it tight.

4. Pull the yarn to the next stick. Wrap it under and around the stick.

5 Wrap the yarn from stick to stick. Always wrap under the sticks. This will make the front side flat.

6 You can change the yarn. Tie the yarn to a stick. Cut it off close to the knot. Tie on the new yarn.

7 Keep wrapping until the sticks are almost covered. Make a final wrap. Tie the yarn to the stick. Cut the yarn about 6 inches (15 cm) from the knot.

8 Cover the end of the stick with glue. Wrap the end of the yarn over the glue. Cover the whole end of the stick. Cut off any extra yarn.

9 Make a **loop** of yarn. Tie it to the end across from the wrapped end. Hang up your god's eye!

PAPER FLOWERS

Make colorful flowers for your room or to give to someone special.

WHAT YOU NEED
• tissue paper
• ruler
• scissors
• chenille stems

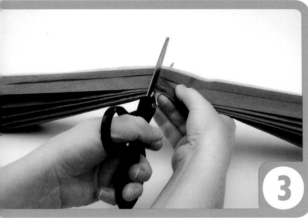

1 Put four pieces of tissue paper in a **stack**.

2 Make a 1-inch (3 cm) fold in the short end. Turn the stack over. Fold it 1 inch (3 cm) again. Keep folding back and forth.

3 Stop when the whole stack is folded into a strip. Cut the folded strip in half.

4 Use a scissors to round off the corners of each strip.

14

5 Wrap a chenille stem around the middle of a strip. Twist it tight.

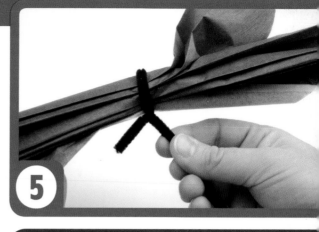

6 Fan out the tissue. Do it slowly and carefully! Pull on one layer at a time. Remember there are four layers. Keep pulling until it looks pretty!

7 Make a second flower with the other strip. Repeat steps 5 and 6.

8 Make a bunch of flowers. Put them in a vase! You can make smaller flowers too. Just use smaller pieces of tissue.

AZTEC SUN

Hang an Aztec sun to symbolize the sun's importance!

1 Place the larger bowl upside down on the foam. Put it at least 2 inches (5 cm) from the sides of the foam.

2 Use the pencil to draw triangles all around the bowl. These are the sun's rays.

3 Remove the bowl. Put the smaller bowl upside down in the middle of the sun. Trace around it.

4 Cut around the outside of the sun. Fold the sun in half. Make a small cut in the middle. Unfold it and cut from the middle to the circle. Cut around the circle.

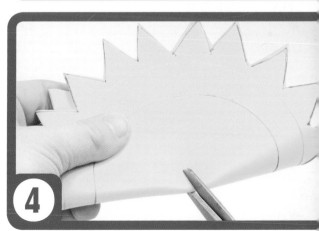

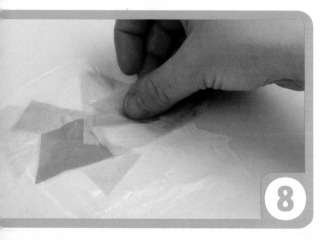

5 Cut small pieces of tissue paper. Make them different sizes and shapes. Use different colors.

6 Tear off a piece of wax paper. It should be bigger than the sun.

7 Put some Mod Podge on the wax paper. Spread it out with the foam brush. Cover an area larger than the sun's center.

8 Lay the pieces of tissue paper on the wet Mod Podge. Overlap them so they cover the Mod Podge completely.

9 Dip the foam brush in some Mod Podge. Gently brush the Mod Podge over the tissue paper. Let it dry.

10 Decorate the sun. Use puffy paint and glitter glue. Let the paint and glue dry completely.

11 Put the foam circle in the middle of the tissue paper. Hold the tissue paper and circle together. Cut around the circle. Cut about ½ inch (1 cm) from the edge.

12 Turn the sun over. Put glue around the edge of the center. Press the tissue paper over the glue. It should cover the center of the sun.

13 Punch a hole in one of the rays. Tie a piece of string through the hole. Hang the sun in a window!

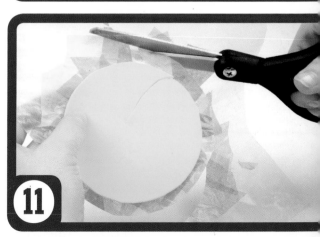

19

HOJaLata

Create colorful tin ornaments.

WHAT YOU NEED
- aluminum pan
- paper
- pencil
- permanent markers
- scissors
- newspaper
- hole punch
- jump rings
- string

1. Place the pan on a piece of paper. Trace around the bottom of the pan.

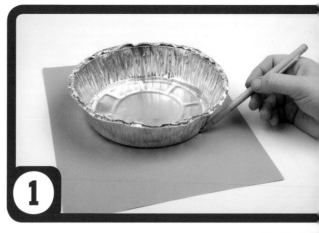

2. Draw your **design** in the circle. Use a black marker. Cut out the circle. Then cut out the bottom of the pan.

3. Put several layers of newspaper on the table. Lay the drawing on the pie pan circle. Trace over the design with a dull pencil. Push hard enough to mark the metal. But be careful not to make holes in it.

4. Turn the metal over. Color in the design with permanent markers.

5. Make more ornaments. Punch a hole in the top and bottom of each one. Connect them with jump rings. Tie string to the top ornament. Use the string to hang up your decoration.

DAY OF THE DEAD BANNER

Make a banner to honor someone who has died.

WHAT YOU NEED
- felt
- paper
- pencil
- scissors
- glue
- puffy paint
- glitter glue
- decorative gems
- hole punch
- string
- cardboard

22

1. Draw a **skull** on a piece of paper. Cut it out. Trace around the paper skull on white felt. Cut it out.

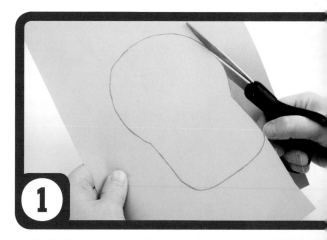

2. Glue the felt skull to a piece of colored felt. Draw the eyes, nose, and teeth.

3. Decorate the banner. Use puffy paint and glitter glue. Add decorative gems. Let the paint and glue dry.

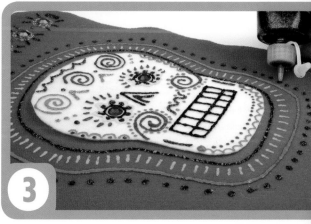

4. Punch holes in the top corners of the banner. Put a string through one hole from front to back. Then put the string through the other hole from back to front. Tie the ends together.

5. Cut a strip of cardboard that fits between the holes. Glue the cardboard on top of the string. Let the glue dry. Hang up your banner!

CINCO DE MAYO PONCHO

This holiday celebrates Mexican victory over the French in 1862.

1. Fold the fleece once into a triangle.

2. Put masking tape along the open sides. The tape should be 2 inches (5 cm) from the edge.

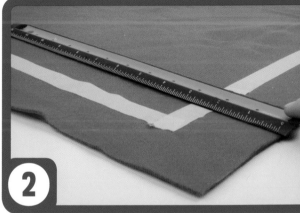

3. Make **fringe** along the open sides. Cut from the edge to the tape. The cuts should be about ½ inch (1 cm) apart. Be sure to cut through both layers of fleece.

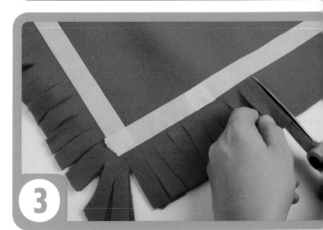

4. Place the bowl in the center of the folded edge. Half of the bowl should be on the fleece. Use a marker to trace a half circle onto the fleece.

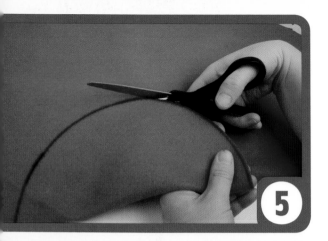

5 Cut around the half circle. Cut on the outside of the line. Make sure you cut through both layers.

6 Cut nine squares out of felt. Make them about 2 inches (5 cm). Cut four of them in half to make triangles. Use one color or different colors.

7 Glue the squares and triangles above the tape. Put a square in the corner. Put two squares on each side. Put triangles next to the side squares.

8 Cut birds or other shapes out of felt. Glue them to the poncho. Use a marker to draw **details**.

9 Let the glue dry completely. Then remove the tape. Your poncho is ready to wear!

26

PARTY Piñata

Make a paper bag piñata for your next party!

WHAT YOU NEED
- large paper bag
- candy
- newspaper
- stapler
- colored tissue paper
- scissors
- glue
- ruler
- markers
- construction paper
- hole punch
- string

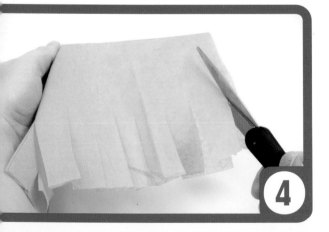

1 Put the candy in the bag. Add crumpled newspaper to fill the bag. Fold the top of the bag two times. Staple it shut.

2 Cover the bottom of the bag with tissue paper. Fold it around the bag like you're wrapping a present. Glue it to the bag.

3 Cut a sheet of tissue paper in half. Fold one of the halves in half.

4 Make **fringe** along the edge opposite the fold. Cut about halfway across the paper. The cuts should be about ½ inch (1 cm) apart.

28

5 Repeat steps 3 and 4 until you have about 20 strips of **fringe**.

6 Put glue along the folded edge of a fringe strip. Glue it to the bag. Start near the bottom with the fringe hanging down.

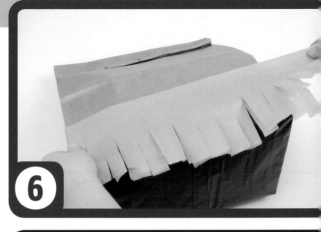

7 Put another strip of fringe over the first one. Keep adding fringe until the bag is covered. Make more fringe strips if necessary.

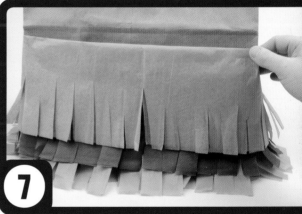

8 Make your piñata into an animal! Draw an animal's face on a piece of construction paper. Cut it out. Glue the face to the front of the piñata.

9 Cut four strips of paper for the legs. Fold each one back and forth. Cut feet out of paper. Glue one to the end of each leg.

10 Glue two legs to the bottom of the piñata. Glue the other two legs to the sides of the piñata.

11 Punch two holes in the top of the piñata.

12 Cut a piece of string about 3 yards (3 m) long. Fold it in half. Put the string through the holes. Tie the ends together. Your piñata is ready to hang!

How to Play

1 Hang up the piñata. Make sure there is a lot of space around the piñata.

2 Decide who goes first. Tie a blindfold around the player's eyes.

3 Spin the player around at least three times. Stop when the player is facing the piñata.

4 Hand the player a bat or stick. Stand back. The player gets to try to hit the piñata three times. Then it's someone else's turn.

5 Keep taking turns until the piñata breaks open. Pick up the candy as it falls out!

Conclusion

Did you learn about Mexican **culture**? Did you have fun making these art projects? Learning about other cultures is very interesting. You can learn about how people around the world live. Try looking up more **information** about Mexicans!

Glossary

Aztec – a civilization that existed in Mexico from the 1200s to the 1400s.

culture – the ideas, traditions, art, and behaviors of a group of people.

design – a decorative pattern or arrangement.

detail – a small part of something.

fringe – a border made up of hanging strips or threads.

information – the facts known about an event or subject.

jewelry – pretty things, such as rings, necklaces, and bracelets, that you wear for decoration.

loop – a circle made by a rope, string, or thread.

papier-mâché – paper soaked in glue and made into different shapes before drying.

skull – the bones that protect the brain and form the face.

stack – a pile of things placed one on top of the other.